Contents

Words appearing in the text in bold, **like this**, are explained in the Glossary.

The Tudor world

Five hundred years ago the world was a very different place. Europeans were only just realizing that America existed, and they had no idea about Australia. Meanwhile the mighty **Ottoman Turks** were threatening to conquer the whole of Europe itself. England (including the Principality of Wales) and Scotland were separate kingdoms, each with its own royal family.

From 1485 to 1603 the Tudor family ruled over England. We now call that period 'Tudor times', and the men, women and children who lived then 'Tudor people'. Some of these people were very rich. Many more were extremely poor. In this book you can find out what life was like for both sorts of people.

A world unlike ours

Most wealthy Tudor people lived in the southern and eastern counties of England. There were more poor people in the north-western counties and in Wales. Many of the poor lived in villages, doing farm work or making cloth in their own homes for very little pay. Most Tudor people lived in the countryside, but some people lived and worked in towns or big Tudor cities like London, Bristol or Norwich.

It was often hard for the poor to afford things, since the **cost of living** kept going up. Life got harder when there was a bad harvest or when the disease of plague struck. Because the population was growing fast, there were not always enough jobs to go round. This meant that some of the poor became even poorer.

The Tudor family
The Tudor family ruled England and Wales from 1485 to 1603:
King Henry VII (king from 1485 to 1509)
King Henry VIII (king from 1509 to 1547)
King Edward VI (king from 1547 to 1553)
Queen Mary I (queen from 1553 to 1558)
Queen Elizabeth I (queen from 1558 to 1603)